LOVE LETTERS

Also by the author in this series…

1. *Love Letters: Poems about Denial*
2. *Then Will You Love Me?: Poems about Bargaining*
3. *Truth Bombs for Fuckboys: Poems about Anger*
4. *Poetry and Prozac: Poems about Depression*
5. *Peregrination: Poems about Acceptance*

LOVE LETTERS

Poems about Denial

Leah Cass

Soul Revitalization LLC

Copyright © 2023 Leah Cass

All rights reserved. No part of this publication may be reproduced, distributed, or transmitted in any form or by any means without the prior written permission of the publisher, except in the case of brief quotations embodied in critical reviews and certain other noncommercial uses permitted by copyright law.

ISBN: 978-1-960143-06-8

Contents

DEDICATION i

PREFACE ii

QUALITY TIME 1

WORDS OF AFFIRMATION 19

PHYSICAL TOUCH 39

ACTS OF SERVICE 55

GIFTS 73

ACKNOWLEDGMENTS 85

END NOTES 86

ABOUT THE AUTHOR 87

ALSO ABOUT THE AUTHOR 88

Dedication

This book is dedicated to Bill, and all the lifetimes we have lived together, in this life and the past.

Preface

This book is about love in all of its forms.

The waiting.

The wanting.

The growing old together.

The heartbreak.

The grief.

Because you cannot truly know grief if you have never truly known love.

I named it poems about denial because I thought that was hilarious when I was still in the "love is a lie" part of my healing.

I still love the delusion.

QUALITY TIME

brown eyes glistened

with a silent, fiery current

shining, hanging, waiting

in tangerine suffocation

question marks stretching

from here to eternity

Choose Your Own Adventure

Let's dance

In this billowing whirlpool of nothingness

As the not knowing stings us

In the cold winter air

The Harlem Shake

Freedom taunts me
as only time can
each minute ticking closer
to the silk lined casket
dust to dust
how can you truly live when you aren't alive?

It taunts me
Hanging in the air
while I taste its sugary sweetness mixed with formaldehyde
every moment lost
but sixty seconds closer to you
you only get so many dreams

Waiting

hold me

wash me with denial, levee the madness

pull me closer

disregard clarity

dream of futures we don't have

tighter

postpone the bitter frigidity

just a few more minutes

under the covers

Winter

I would love you

just to show you that

we can change course

escape the sins of our fathers

revise infinite destinies

escape this voluntary cage

meet our souls again

I would love you

because I'm reckless

Madness in Dark Rooms

Every time he smiles

my heart collapses

and my brain turns to mush

I lose myself

in the light

Blinded

Maybe we could fall in love again

Under the stars

While the lake laps quietly against the shore

The wind rustles through the branches

I'll still sleep on my side of the bed

It's warmer here

On top of the ashes

On Top of the Ashes

Oh how I love you still
I fall deep into
the colors of your eyes

Hazel

Are there words for
Craving a heaven
That never existed

I have hungered for
The taste of your lips
A thousand days and nights

Fantasies Fashioned
Of bodies twisted

Still I stand at the
Top of the staircase
Beneath the lights

Beneath the Lights

When I look into
You

I see the stars and
The moon and
My unmet potential
Together
Merging in the sky

The electricity
Between us
The truth in your
Eyes

Current

And you hold me

Still

Skin to skin after

I've discarded my day

Eternity

I wish I could
Erase all the mistakes
Of my stupid brain
When I let it do the
Driving

But I know I am
Forever changed
Because our hearts

Collided

This love will

never die

no matter

how many times

I beat it down

and light it

on fire

and stamp it

out

my heart

still beats

for you

Trick Candles

Our paths run parallel

In mirrored vibration

Our minds

Walk the line while

Only our hearts

Cross over

Cross Over

I still love you
When you sweep
The streets at
Midnight and when I
Cry and say you're
Never there and
When it's autumn
And I'm winded
When I'm clothed
And when I'm bare

Always and Forever

*Every broken road has led me
back to you.*

WORDS OF AFFIRMATION

I wish I could

Wash out my brain

With soap and water

When it takes

Your name

In vain

The Third Commandment

He roared like the ocean

And she crashed

In his waves

Riptide

Deliver me

from the

elliptical minutes

of this cocaine

meditation

I discovered

from the fall

you are my

favorite person

Number One Spot

Sun soaked white light
colorful, dreamy
melting into the inky abyss
I'll be your Madonna
I'll be your whore
so simple so complex

So Simple, So Complex

The sun shone

warm, browning my opal skin

and you were there

simple, free

from any complications

my heart skipped so

lightly

Easy, like a Sunday Morning

How many times have my

Tears dried on

Your skin as

Our souls speak in

Silence

Salt of the Earth

I wonder sometimes

If our souls speak

Even while we sleep

5D

I wake up in the morning
Ready for beginnings

More adjusted to the light

And the only vibrations
Left between us

Are the notes of the
Songs that keep
Us up
All night

Routine

Two flickering flames
Dance in perfect unison
Shadows bouncing in the light

Twins

She was the only heaven
He would ever enter
And he was the only sin
She couldn't commit

On Earth

I laid with you

In darkness

Held your hand

And kissed your head

You're the sugar

I've been craving

I'm still crashing

From the high

Diabetes

Every time

I get up to leave

You pull me back

Between the sheets

And I Come

I used to scoff at the women
Who lit themselves on fire
To have a man put them out
Until I met you and saw
My own flames

Shadow Self

Maybe in dreams

We feel so alive

Because in them

We can control

Other people, places, and time

Control

And you were the one
Who made me
Believe in things
I couldn't touch

And I Loved it so Much

But I'm tired of
Begging you to
Remember what
Our souls
Promised each
Other before
We born

Release

I wish instead
I had told you
That I wanted to
Lay in the crack between
Your arms and shoulders
And watch you grow
Slowly

Lady in Waiting

*In one reckless moment I became
forever haunted.*

PHYSICAL TOUCH

Eyes closed

I rest

as I feel

the tickle

of your tongue

across my flesh

Short Sighted

On Sunday mornings

let me sleep

I'll worship at

your body's altar

tie me up

and set me free

I'm Spiritual, not Religious

I'll still worship your body

If you teach me

How to pray

Invocation

Lock your lips

on my hips

dive into me

High

I'll follow you home
we can dance
beneath the moonlight
to yesterday's sweet ode

Heeling

I want you

to go so deep

I can feel

your soul

juxtaposed

on mine

rock in

perfect harmony

let it loop

around and

Intertwine

The Bends

How can these

twisted fantasies grow

tangled in my mind?

How can I now weed

them out and burn

their stump

so sinful, intertwined

Chewing on Pencils and Staring into Space

Slip

Into me

Slowly

Hips pressing

Against hips

Finally

Home

Home

Shall we stay
Twisted in these
Tangled sheets
While the world
Passes quietly by

Sunday

I want to
Journey to the ocean
And let you fuck me
While the waves
Crash over my shoulders
And sand bunches up
Between my thighs

We'll leave our
Impression on the
Soft, smooth earth

If only
For tonight

Beach Bums

He crawled

so deep

inside me

I could feel him

in my marrow

and my blood

was forever

imprinted with

his DNA

Sitting in Parked Cars Outside the Window

You lose yourself too

sometimes and I search

for you in the spray

and foam of the ocean

instead of finding myself

but maybe you will find

me too and we can trade places

souls twisting in motion

Sometimes

Between us there

Is fire in the

Frequency

Burning through

The rubble in

Our Energy and

Melting the ice,

Once

Our legacy

Alchemy

I've been begging you to take me

Naked, Purely, Whole

ACTS OF SERVICE

I have been smiling again

with you beside me, warm

and your scent clinging

to the tips of my hair

as I go about my day

Miracles

I drank you bitter

Like my coffee

And you kept me up

All night

Caffeine

I watched myself
being swept away
by the flow of your river

Caught in the current
my bare breasts bobbed
when I finally stopped

The chill of cold air
has given me fever

But to your force
do I belong

Delta

I could feel his

Poetry rustling

In midnight breezes

Speeding towards me

Again

But I Wasn't Ready

How still

Can I get drunk

Off the libations

Of your smile

When your face has

Faded across the miles

Contact High

Our hearts

Beat in perfect

Unison but our

Brains tell us

They don't exist

Deep In My Heart

I still see your face

In every dark ink blotted

Rorschach card

And I think I'm

Failing the test

Lock Me up and Throw Away the Key

I sometimes wonder

If the stars

Carry the messages

I whisper, twinkling

To your heart

Twinkle, Twinkle

Time stands still

because my patience for you

is infinite

I'll get lost again

without regret

The journey to your heart

my pilgrimage

The Camino de Santiago

I love that our sitting room

smells like tranquility at 2 am

And I can still hear you breathing

over the noise in my head

Incense

I've felt the hunger pangs
of your staggering might
and prayed
you would pick me up
and eat me on the table

Breakfast

Your beard rubbed

against my skin and

in that moment

we were drunk

and real and raw

and the universe

could never be against us

But Maybe It Was

There is

beauty in the

nonsense too

I have walked

A tapered trail

to your house

slowly

just a human

wasting all my time

Meandering

Writers can make any cliché romantic
even when the fires burn out
and the moon is black
and the tide has retreated
Back into the ocean

There are plenty of Fish in the Sea

I'm drunk off the power
of your raw desire
If you beckon me close
I promise to come near

Power Play

There is grief in your kindness

I can see it in your eyes

We have danced and broken

and healed

A Hundred Thousand Times

GIFTS

If peace exists

you gave me this

with just a kiss

With Just a Kiss

Unopened gifts gifted
lay bare beneath the tree

Will You Ever Unwrap Me?

I love that
I can fall asleep knowing
you will still love me
in the morning

I can roll over and rest my head and
you'll softly stroke my chest
Your hands whisper I can be still now
It wasn't just a dream

Security

I'll leave this

Suitcase packed

a testament

To the apparitions

Of these other possible futures

Timelines

There is even beauty

in the red lipstick-stained mistakes

in staring at you through this cloudy haze

of cigarette smoke and pheromones

A loose majestic tiger of raw desire

waiting to pounce

Wild Cats

Music notes

Wafted into my ears

So sweet, so consonant

And once

You were mine

If only for a moment

If Only for A Moment

Teach me again

what it means to feel alive

Remind me who I was

before all these tears I've cried

Build me a Time Machine

I've always had
a penchant for potential
existing only in
the world of dreams

Ephemeral

I wish I could

Draw every line

And wrinkle

Crossing your face

But the true art lies

Between us

In the negative space

Negative Space

I stayed awake for you, baby
while the candle burned out
and my eyelids got heavy and
the birds started to chirp

And you showed up
to stare as I slept
I saw you in dreams
but you had already left

Missed Connections Part 2

I still hope to see
You at the end of this road
Smiling, wishing, too

Two

Acknowledgments

I would not be anywhere without my family. Thank you to Bill, Kaylee, Eliza, Vanessa, William, Jason, and Lois. Huge thank you to Aimee, who helped me edit and format and calmed me down when I needed it. Special shout out to Instagram as well, and all the followers who believed in me when I was just sad and trying to feel better. Thank you to my soul family, for believing in me and always encouraging me. And thank you to my dad. I wish you were still here to see it.

End Notes

1. This series is an homage to the five stages of grief model was developed by **Elisabeth Kübler-Ross,** and became famous after she published her book On Death and Dying in 1969.

2. Chapters are based on the five love languages, developed by Gary Chapman.

3. Page 13- Please tell me I'm not the only one who remembers these books?

4. Page 31- "You shall not take the name of the Lord your God in vain." (Exodus 20:7) – The Third Commandment

5. Page 33 – LUDA – a reference to Ludacris

6. Page 34- The Madonna-Whore Complex, a psychological condition where heterosexual men place women into categories of suitable for sexual arousal vs suitable for marriage.

7. Pages 35 – Hearts to Lionel Richie

8. Page 75 - ***The Camino de Santiago*** is a famous pilgrimage many take in Spain and on my personal bucket list.

About The Author

Leah Cass is a poet, writer, mental health advocate, and lover of all things spiritual. She currently resides in Pittsburgh, PA with her husband, daughter, and two spoiled cats. She graduated from Chatham University with a bachelor's degree in Psychology and continued her education in clinical mental health counseling at Duquesne University.

A strong believer in the power of story to build community and spark healing, Leah loves using her voice to help others open up about their own experiences with mental health and personal growth. She frequently speaks at events and workshops on topics such as mental health awareness, post traumatic growth, and self-care. You can find her on Instagram as @elleunchained.

Also About The Author

Made in the USA
Middletown, DE
19 March 2024